Winter Prayer Journal

Ecclesiastes 3:1-8
A Season for Everything

1 There is a time for everything, and a season for every activity under the heavens:

2 A time to be born and a time to die, a time to plant and a time to uproot,

3 a time to kill and a time to heal, a time to tear down and a time to build,

4 a time to weep and a time to laugh, a time to mourn and a time to dance,

5 a time to scatter stones and a time to gather them, a time to embrace and a time to refrain from embracing,

6 a time to search and a time to give up, a time to keep and a time to throw away,

7 a time to tear and a time to mend, a time to be silent and a time to speak,

8 a time to love and a time to hate, a time for war and a time for peace.

Winter brings a lot of different emotions to mind for different people. Some look forward to the snow, sledding, and skiing, warming oneself by a cozy fire, and drinking warm drinks with family and friends.

Others dread the cold and inclement weather, fewer daylight hours, scraping ice off windshields and driveways, dangerous driving conditions, and higher incidences of illness.

Regardless of your attitude toward winter, it is one of the four seasons that God intentionally created as part of the rhythm of nature's cycles.

There is immaculate beauty in a mountaintop freshly covered in snow, in the intricately designed structure of each individual snowflake, and the pure whiteness of snow-covered fields. This beauty is a gift from God.

At the start of winter we have the season of Advent which is the time of preparation and expectation that leads up to Christmas Day. The word "Advent" comes from the Latin word adventus, which means "coming". Advent is a time to reflect on the sacred meaning of Christmas and to renew hope. Advent is a time to celebrate our faith.

During winter there is the season of Lent. Lent is a 40-day period of preparation and reflection leading up to Easter. It is a time to remember Jesus's sacrifice and the events leading up to his crucifixion, and to prepare for Easter's celebration of his resurrection.

It begins on Ash Wednesday and ends on Easter Eve.

Some practices during Lent include:

Giving things up

Self-discipline.

Prayer:

Studying the Bible

Helping those in need

The word "Lent" comes from an old English word meaning "lengthen" because it happens during the time of year when the days start to get longer.

Ecclesiastes 3: 1
"There is a time for everything, and a season for every activity under heaven"

Do you consider yourself to be in the winter of your life?

The Winter of Age.

Remember what was written in Ecclesiastes and the message behind those words encourage us to live this season of life even though it is the winter, with all the activity we can and still glorify God in any way we can.

Proverbs 16: 31
"Grey hair is a crown of splendour; it is attained by a righteous life."

Facing Life's Winter

Job 12: 12
"Is not wisdom found among the aged? Does not long life bring about understanding?"

Psalm 92: 12 – 15
"The righteous will flourish like the palm tree, they will grow like a cedar of Lebanon, planted in the house of the Lord, they will flourish

in the courts of our God. They will still bear fruit in old age, they will stay fresh and green, proclaiming, "The Lord is upright, he is my Rock and there is no wickedness in him."

Reflections for Winter

A time for preparation
Winter can be a time to prepare for the busy seasons ahead by spending time in prayer, in the Word of God, and in fellowship. It can also be a time to consider your spiritual life and preparation for Advent and Lent.

A time to trust in God
God gives us seasons to help us build trust in Him and to develop into better people. During winter storms, we can turn to God for deliverance.

A time to appreciate God's gifts
Winter can be a time to reflect on God's good gifts to us, such as His generosity and faithfulness.

A time to experience God's presence
Winter can be a time when God often feels silent, but He is still near. Christmas is a time when we remember the gift of the birth of Jesus Christ.

A time for rest
Winter can be a time for rest, where we can allow our bodies and minds to rest and ready ourselves for the busy seasons ahead.

A time of spiritual comfort
Winter can feel dark, gloomy and cold. It's a time to hunker down, retreat from the hectic pace of life, pause and reflect. We seek out physical comforts like hot soup or hot chocolate. We can draw spiritual comforts by slowing down from the hectic pace and demands of life and leaning into God of all comfort, seeking His contentment.

Be still and know I am God – Psalm 46:10

Winter reminds us of the sovereignty and power of God as we are reminded that He is in control of our lives just as He controls the wintery weather around us. Snow is also a powerful symbol of the purity and holiness of God. God reveals Himself in many different ways through the season of winter.

Our spiritual lives can also enter a time that feels like winter, a season in which God feels distant even when we seek Him through worship, reading His word, and prayer. During these times we may feel immersed in darkness, loneliness, and solitude, or a sense of hopelessness or despair from the difficult times through which we are walking.

The Bible uses winter as a symbol to describe how we grow spiritually, experience new beginnings and trust in God's constant presence in every part of our lives. These verses below help us understand the purpose in every challenge and God's unwavering presence through it all.

Whether you are curious to see what the Bible has to say about the season of winter and cold weather or you are desperately searching for help and wisdom during this personal season of a spiritual winter, use these Bible verses about winter to teach you and encourage you about what God has to say about this unique season.

Winter is one of the seasons God created in His sovereignty over all things to create order and structure for all of creation. He created day and night, cold and heat, summer and winter, a time to plant and a time to harvest all with the intent of blessing us.

Some may love the cold and snow, while others may look forward to the time when the temperatures increase and the ice begins to melt but regardless we can trust that the seasons are a beautiful part of God's plan for our world.

Expect spiritual winters: Prepare for them so they feel less devastating.

Winter can be a time when God's work is happening, even if it doesn't feel like it. It can also be a time to build trust in God and develop into a better person and a better Christian.

We should acknowledge the Winter of the Soul and set aside time to Thrive in the Winter Season of the Soul

Psalm 130:5 – 6
In the winter of his soul the psalmist wrote, "I wait for the Lord, my soul waits, and in His word I put my hope.
My soul waits for the Lord more than watchmen wait for the morning"

Ecclesiastes 3:1-2 – Winter Reminds Us of God's Timing

There is a time for everything, and a season for every activity under the heavens: a time to be born and a time to die, a time to plant and a time to uproot – Ecclesiastes 3:1-2

God has declared that there is a time and purpose for everything that occurs on the earth, and the seasons of nature were established for a reason. In each season there is beauty and God is revealing Himself to us in different ways.

Although some view the cold and dreary days of winter as a time of bitterness and death, God also uses winter to allow nature to rest and be re-energized for the bursting forth of new life.

The glittery snow displays God's purity and beauty in refreshing ways. God is accomplishing specific purposes in the winter season, and soon enough it will be time for spring to burst forth.

Isaiah 53:6
All we like sheep have gone astray; we have turned everyone to his own way

December

1st **December**

The Christian year begins not with the great feasts of Christmas, Easter or Pentecost but with waiting. Advent is in many ways a stark season - a time to be in touch with our deepest desires and needs.

It is a season of longing directed towards Christ, revealed as God-with-us, Emmanuel.

Advent is a season of waiting, but in hope and in expectation.

Use this season of Advent to challenge your inner spiritual life and by doing so challenge your outer life in your thoughts and actions. Challenge your inner life through spiritual prompts and pathways to prayer.

Advent Goals

What do I want from Advent?
What am I anticipating?
What answer, longing or hope am I waiting for?
How will this Advent change my inner and outer Christian life?

2nd December

The word "Advent" is derived from the Latin word adventus, meaning "coming,"

During Advent we think about hope, faith, joy, and peace.

Use this time of Advent through practicing spiritual disciplines to heal your hurts, grow your faith and move closer to God. In doing so challenge your outer life into helping those without homes and those in need.

Have I left enough space in the busy Advent season to pay attention, to listen, to wait, and to be surprised?

What practical steps can I take to both guard those quiet moments but also embrace divine interruptions?

3rd December

Advent is a time of reflection and contemplation with God.

It is a time to create space in our lives to welcome Christ.

Preparing for Advent
How can I serve this Advent season?

This Advent you are invited to give your time, talents, and treasure to a cause that means something to you. When those who love God work together, great things happen.

Deuteronomy 15:10
You shall give to him freely, and your heart shall not be grudging when you give to him, because for this the Lord your God will bless you in all your work and in all that you undertake.

4th December

Spiritual Prompts for Advent

1. Have I left enough space in the busy holiday season to pay attention, to listen, to wait, and to be surprised? What practical steps can I take to both guard those quiet moments but also embrace divine interruptions?

2. What are some ways I can share God's love with others during Advent?

3. How did I best serve God this year?

4. How do I find more time to pray?

5. What are the blessings in my life that I sometimes take for granted?

6. How can I prepare myself, my home, and my family for the arrival of Jesus in a way that nurtures a spirit of anticipation and hope?

7. What am I most grateful for in my life right now?

8. How can I deepen my prayer life during the Advent season?

9. What is one thing I can do to show kindness to others today and each day of Advent?

10. How am I being called to serve others in my community this Advent?

5th **December**

Faith

Are you lacking in faith?

How can you strengthen your faith?

Reach Out to Others
While Advent is a time for inner reflection, focusing solely on ourselves tempts us to neglect our call to be good neighbours.

The bible speaks very directly about how our faith must ultimately result in action: "Faith of itself, if it does not have works, is dead." James 2:17

Turning our inward Advent reflections into outward actions shows that God is truly working in our lives.

6th **December**

Spiritual Prompts for Advent

1. What are my biggest fears, and how can I trust in God to help me overcome them?

2. Consider the effects of light. It can warm and it can guide, but it can also expose and surprise. What does light in the darkness mean for you in your life this Advent and for the world?

3. How can I create more peace in my life and in the world around me this Advent?

4. What lessons have I learned from the challenging experiences I've had this year?

5. What is one way I can let go of worry and trust in God more?

6. What are some things I need to forgive others for, and how can I work towards compassion?

7. How have I seen God at work in my life recently, and how can I be more aware of His presence?

8. What are my hopes for my spiritual growth in the coming year?

9. How can I serve God this Advent season?

10. When I wake up on Christmas morning, how will I be different? How do I hope the meditations and practices of the season will shape me?

7th **December**

Hoping

When you thought you had lost your path, beneath all your fears, I am there

When meaning is gone

I am that meaning

When truth seems hard to find,

I am that truth

When even love seems a bitter thing

I will take that bitter cup from you

And you will taste the wine of my forgiveness

Come back with me to the centre of the things and be held, not torn

Each day is an opportunity for hope

And hope will often arise from those deemed hopeless

Learn to hope in God even when hope seems impossible and beyond

Learn to hope in God's grace even when the rules of the world cry out that your values have no currency

Learn to hope in God's love

Hope as tender and ephemeral as a new shoot

But which can make the desert bloom and the song birds return.

Richard Carter The City is my Monastery – A contemporary rule of life.

Hope

What hopes have you this Advent?

8th December

Advent: Peace - Isaiah 40:3-5

"A voice of one calling: "In the wilderness prepare the way for the LORD ; make straight in the desert a highway for our God. Every valley shall be raised up, every mountain and hill made low; the rough ground shall become level, the rugged places a plain. And the glory of the LORD will be revealed, and all people will see it together. For the mouth of the LORD has spoken."

Let this Advent be a time of peace for you.

Colossians 3:15 says, "Let the peace of Christ rule in your hearts, since as members of one body you were called to peace. And be thankful."

During Advent, we can turn off the noise – the news, the socials, the music – and just sit in silence before God.

Tell God what you are waiting for this Advent.

9th December

At Advent we welcome, wait, recognise and embrace God's coming. Events such as a boiling climate and raging wars have created an unsettled world. This Advent we focus on God's coming as the Prince of PEACE.

Pray

Lord, I invite your peace to rule my heart! As I end this year and reflect on your many gifts you have given me; let my heart be encouraged with the truth that you are a good God. I thank you for sending your Son to die for me. I thank you for the peace I have through you. May my words and actions be ones that glorify you. Amen.

What is getting in the way of feeling at peace?

10th **December**

Joy
What brings you joy? Make a list.
How can you bring joy to others?

Advent Reflections

11th December

Isaiah 55:10 – Promise of God's Word and Provision
"As the rain and the snow come down from heaven, and do not return to it without watering the earth and making it bud and flourish, so that it yields seed for the sower and bread for the eater."

This verse beautifully captures the essence of winter's role in nature's cycle. Just as snow nourishes the earth, God's Word enriches our souls, ensuring spiritual growth and nourishment. The imagery of snow in this verse is a reminder of the silent but profound impact of God's promises in our lives, much like the unseen growth beneath the winter snow.

12th **December**

Winter Prayer Walking

Let's Go for a Walk

Many Christians pray while walking, and prayer walking is a spiritual practice that can take many forms.

Ephesians 5:2

"and walk in the way of love, just as Christ loved us and gave himself up for us as a fragrant offering and sacrifice to God."

For many the rhythmic slap of our feet on the ground and the movement of our whole bodies frees us to pray.

13th December

Isaiah 28:2 – The Lord is a Crown of Glory
"Behold, the Lord has one who is mighty and strong; like a storm of hail, a destroying tempest, like a storm of mighty, overflowing waters, he casts down to the earth with his hand."

14th December

Winter Prayer Walking

Praying while walking integrates our bodies with our minds and spirits.

Walking with God is a lifelong journey of growing intimacy, obedience and transformation.

As we seek His presence, depend on His guidance and persevere in faith, we experience the joy and fulfilment of a relationship with God.

Micah 6:8

"He has shown you, O mortal, what is good.

And what does the Lord require of you?

To act justly and to love mercy and to walk humbly with your God."

If you are preoccupied, upset or angry about something set out on a walk. Pray as you walk and discover the power of praying while walking.

When you get home your perspective will change. That brief time with God on a walk will expand to represent the long faith journey of your life.

Prayer walking gets us out of our heads and out of our houses so we can pray with our whole body in God's creation.

While prayer walking we can see the glories of winter.

15th December

Genesis 8:22 – God Created Seasons As Part of His Sovereign Plan
"As long as the earth endures, seedtime and harvest, cold and heat, summer and winter, day and night will never cease."

Light-Triggered Prayers

From now until after Christmas, we'll see extra lights just about everywhere—strung over trees, shrubbery, posts and poles, rooflines, and so on.

When your attention is attracted to Advent lights, pray something like, "God, may your light be present in me today." Or, "Jesus, may your love in my life create light for others."

Make up whatever short prayer you want. Allow that light-related phrase to be triggered whenever lights shine on you.

16th December

A popular tradition at Advent is marking the progression of the season through an Advent wreath
made up of five candles.

This symbol is borrowed from the emphasis in the Bible of Jesus being the Light of the World (Matt. 4:16; John 1:4–9; 8:12).

Each week, a new candle is lit in anticipation of Christmas Eve.

The last candle, called the Christ Candle, is lit on Christmas Eve to represent Jesus' first advent.

Through this theme of ever-increasing light penetrating the darkness, we can see the symbol of God overwhelming the darkness in the world and in our lives.

Hymn Phrases

When you hear a Christmas carol, pay attention to the words, and just hold onto a phrase or two for your prayer during the morning's commute or chores around the house.

For instance, maybe you're hearing an instrumental version of "Away in a Manger," a song usually relegated in our minds to the category of children's songs. But here's the final verse to reflect upon.

'Be near me, Lord Jesus, I ask you to stay
close by me forever and love me, I pray.

Bless all the dear children in thy tender care
and fit us for heaven to live with thee there.'

17th **December**

The season of Advent is one of joy, light and beauty, but sometimes it is overwhelming, dark and hard.

Let God's light shine into this season. The power of God's Word is available to help light the way.

Prayer can bring peace during this frantic Christmas season.

Isaiah 9:2

The people who walked in darkness have seen a great light; those who lived in a land of deep darkness—on them light has shined."

18th **December**

Faith

Are you lacking in faith?

How can you strengthen your faith?

How do I hope the meditations and practices of the season of Advent will shape me?

19th **December**

Advent: Joy - Isaiah 12:2-6
"Surely God is my salvation; I will trust and not be afraid. The LORD, the LORD himself, is my strength and my defense ; he has become my salvation." With joy you will draw water from the wells of salvation. In that day you will say: "Give praise to the LORD, proclaim his name; make known among the nations what he has done, and proclaim that his name is exalted. Sing to the LORD, for he has done glorious things; let this be known to all the world. Shout aloud and sing for joy, people of Zion, for great is the Holy One of Israel among you."

20th **December**

Are you at a crossroads in your life?
Advent provides a space for people at a crossroads in life to pause, step back and reflect on where they are, the questions they need to answer, what they really want and how to take steps forward.

Jeremiah 6:16
"Stand at the crossroads and look. Look for the ancient paths. Ask where the good way is and walk in it and you will find rest for your soul."

The crossroads could be vocational, such as a career change, or relational, such as divorce or separation. It could be a significant interruption in life from a change of circumstances or health, or simply a sense of wanting something different from life.

21st December

During this solemn season of Advent in which the Church bids us prepare to celebrate the coming of Christ;
a coming that we recall in the Child of Bethlehem;
a coming that we experience in the gift of his Spirit, in the bread of the Eucharist, in the joy of human lives that are shared;
a coming we wait for when God gathers up all things in Christ.

Let us turn towards the light and as we turn towards the light, let us have on our hearts all those who see no light, for whom all is darkness and despair.

Let us pray that they too may be illumined by Christ who is our light.

Thoughts and Prayers

22nd December

Some churches have a 'Blue Christmas' service just before Christmas.

The 'Blue Christmas' service is a recognition and a public assurance that Christmas is emphatically not about enforced jollity or pressure to be 'on form'. But an equal assurance that in celebrating the incarnation, there is, in the words of the old carol, 'comfort and joy' that is possible when the ancient wisdom of Scripture bursts into life with the shocking gospel that God is with us.

Pray
For the gifts I have.
For forgiveness for my sins of negligence, ignorance and wilful self-interest.
I offer all that I have.
I repent.
I am determined to change.

23rd December

Matthew 5:16
In the same way, let your light shine before others, that they may see your good deeds and glorify your Father in heaven.

Light is used to symbolise God, faith, and holiness throughout the Bible. As Christians, we are called to not only walk in the light but to be the light for others.

24th December

Christmas Eve

Sacrament is incarnation
God bearers

He came to the midnight Mass on Christmas Eve

I saw him from the clergy vestry window
He was a single man with dark olive skin and a beard
He had a thick jacket pulled up around his ears and shadowed eyes
But it was the large shapeless pack on his back that raised my suspicions
We have all seen the photos of the perpetrators of terror in our newspapers
Those seemingly innocent young faces with soft features that have packed explosives together with nails and other brutal shrapnel
Where was this lone man from – I had no way of knowing
Perhaps the Middle East – Syria or Afghanistan or Iraq or Libya –
or perhaps North African – Algeria or Morocco
or perhaps even Bangladesh or Northern Pakistan
We are told repeatedly to be alert. But was I being foolish or needlessly stereotyping?
Something about the way he was carrying the pack on his back was unusual
I am attentive to these signs. Who in this day and age in a crowded central London building is not? You look out for people who for whatever reason don't seem to fit
He was not one of many homeless visitors – his clothes were too chosen, they were not ones he had slept with on the streets. And yet alone. No one with him, no group
And why that oddly shaped backpack?
I came to take a closer look
Down the stairs and along the north aisle
As I came towards him our eyes met and he shifted the pack on his back as though it were something heavy which needed protecting – a precious cargo or worse
And as I came closer and he turned away
And then I saw them – two feet and tiny shoes and then the child's

head which I had not seen before nestling on his father's neck
And I heard a cry and I realized this father had turned to comfort the child he was carrying so tenderly that father and child seemed one
And I felt joy and instant relief
He was carrying his son – this precious backpack was a life – not death
In the place of fear and suspicion – a baby
God's salvation
God's Eucharist
God's love for the world
Calling us into that same story
Of carrying love
Of being the God bearers
The peace of Christ carried on his father's back.

Richard Carter   The City is my Monastery – A contemporary rule of life
'Our place of retreat, our monastery, is here and now, where we are today'

25th December

MERRY CHRISTMAS

Luke 2:1–7
In those days a decree went out from Caesar Augustus that all the world should be registered. This was the first registration when Quirinius was governor of Syria. And all went to be registered, each to his own town. And Joseph also went up from Galilee, from the town of Nazareth, to Judea, to the city of David, which is called Bethlehem, because he was of the house and lineage of David, to be registered with Mary, his betrothed, who was with child. And while they were there, the time came for her to give birth. And she gave birth to her firstborn son and wrapped him in swaddling cloths and laid him in a manger, because there was no place for them in the inn.

Isaiah 9:6: "For to us a child is born, to us a son is given, and the government will be on his shoulders. And he will be called Wonderful Counsellor, Mighty God, Everlasting Father, Prince of Peace."

Luke 2:8-20

8 And there were shepherds living out in the fields nearby, keeping watch over their flocks at night. 9 An angel of the Lord appeared to them, and the glory of the Lord shone around them, and they were terrified. 10 But the angel said to them, "Do not be afraid. I bring you good news that will cause great joy for all the people. 11 Today in the town of David a Savior has been born to you; he is the Messiah, the Lord. 12 This will be a sign to you: You will find a baby wrapped in cloths and lying in a manger."

13 Suddenly a great company of the heavenly host appeared with the angel, praising God and saying,

14 "Glory to God in the highest heaven,
   and on earth peace to those on whom his favour rests."

15 When the angels had left them and gone into heaven, the shepherds said to one another, "Let's go to Bethlehem and see this thing that has happened, which the Lord has told us about."

16 So they hurried off and found Mary and Joseph, and the baby, who was lying in the manger. 17 When they had seen him, they spread the word concerning what had been told them about this child, 18 and all who heard it were amazed at what the shepherds said to them. 19 But Mary treasured up all these things and pondered them in her heart. 20 The shepherds returned, glorifying and praising God for all the things they had heard and seen, which were just as they had been told.

26th December

Boxing Day

St Stephen's Day

Today, as the Christmas carol describes it, is the 'Feast of Stephen' or St Stephen's Day, also known as Boxing Day.

If we've been fortunate enough to have had a Christmas Day with good food and company, then Boxing Day or St Stephen's Day can feel a bit of an anticlimax. The boxes of boxing day come from a time when servants were given the day off after cooking for the celebrations of their masters, and given a box of treats to take home to their own families.

Today we think about those unsung heroes who just gets on with it: our local communities and societies are enriched hugely by people who do that, running sports clubs or lunch clubs, after school activities or dementia cafes. People who help knit us together, give us somewhere to be, help us eat together or make friends, build community and give a helping hand to someone else who needs it today.

A message of today: it's about living a life that puts others needs before our own.

Pray

So come now, Child of Bethlehem, to strengthen me in these days.
May I feel your presence in a way I have never known, not just as one born in a stable long ago and far away but as the One born in my heart.

Today, Loving God I remember the unsung heroes in my community. I name some of them to you now. Thank you for their work and their presence. They are the salt of the earth. Please God, help me to live a life that puts the needs of others before my own.

27th December

John : Chapter 1

In the beginning was the Word, and the Word was with God, and the Word was God. He was in the beginning with God. All things came into being through him, and without him not one thing came into being. What has come into being in him was life, and the life was the light of all people. The light shines in the darkness, and the darkness did not overtake it.

There was a man sent from God whose name was John. He came as a witness to testify to the light, so that all might believe through him. He himself was not the light, but he came to testify to the light. The true light, which enlightens everyone, was coming into the world.

He was in the world, and the world came into being through him, yet the world did not know him. He came to what was his own, and his own people did not accept him. But to all who received him, who believed in his name, he gave power to become children of God, who were born, not of blood or of the will of the flesh or of the will of man, but of God.

And the Word became flesh and lived among us, and we have seen his glory, the glory as of a father's only son, full of grace and truth.

28th December

Psalm 37:23-24 "The LORD makes firm the steps of the one who delights in him; though he may stumble, he will not fall, for the LORD upholds him with his hand."

Have I lost my way?

Sometimes something happens to us that turns our life upside down. It feels that along our life's journey, we have 'lost our way'.

There are times when we become aware that the way we are living our lives no longer feels quite right. We may experience a mixture of emotions – perhaps we feel directionless, life feels a bit pointless and we lack that zest for life we used to have when we were younger.

Or perhaps we find ourselves overwhelmed. Maybe we sense there is more to us than we know, we have potential that is not being fully realised.

These feelings can be upsetting but they can also be the most fertile times in our lives. It is time to stop, look and listen to God. We need to take time to reflect.

Pray and ask: what does God want for me?

29th December

Winter Prayer Walking

Be Attentive to God's Voice:

Listen for God's guidance as you walk. Sometimes, God will put specific people or situations on your heart to pray for.

Isaiah 30:21

"Whether you turn to the right or to the left, your ears will hear a voice behind you, saying, "This is the way; walk in it."

Set out around your local neighbourhood and begin your walk with a simple prayer, like "Come, Holy Spirit", to centre yourself, to mark this as something more than a dander and to open yourself up to what Jesus may say and do through your intercession.

Consider what catches your attention as you walk and bring your reflections to Jesus in conversational prayer. Ask Him simple questions like, "Jesus, what do you see and what do you say?"

Psalm 37:23

The steps of those who pursue God follow firmly in the footsteps of the Lord, and God delights in every step they take to follow him.

Notice what Jesus has revealed to you, what you feel around certain spaces and consider how you can respond through your actions and ongoing prayer.

2 Corinthians 5:7

"For we walk by faith, not by sight."

See the people you pass

The lives they carry

The stories in their faces

The fragments of conversation you catch

See the person

The depth and the richness and mystery of our humanity

The beauty and uniqueness of each face

Let this humanity also be your prayer

Each and every person made in the image of God

Each person known by the Creator

Each person loved by the Creator.

Be filled with compassion

Let this walking be your offering

Let this walking be your prayer

30th December

Almighty God, let us not be overwhelmed by the enormity of the world's suffering:
Let us do justly now, walk humbly now, and love mercy now, for we are not expected to complete this work, but neither are we free to abandon it.

Transform our fear, anger, sorrow, and shame into prayers, and fill those prayers with wisdom and courage, turn this wisdom and courage into compassion that inspires works of love, so that your ways of justice, peace and mercy may be known in our lives and in the life of the world.
Amen.

Here are some Christian prompts for New Year's goals:

Reflect on the past year
Consider what you learned, what hardships you faced, and when you felt God's presence.

Identify areas for growth

Consider where you can have the most impact in the coming year, such as a relationship, project, or ministry.

Develop a heart of worship
Consider how you can incorporate God's peace into your home and life.

Give your time and service to the Lord
Consider how you can make a difference at home, work, church, and other places.

Praise God for your blessings
Consider how your achievements and blessings are a reflection of God's presence, and give praise to God for all that you have.

Lessons from Looking Back

31st December

We are on the other side now of Christ's birth.
Advent can be looked at as a season to look back and one to look forward—preparing for Jesus' second coming.

As you look back over **December** what did the season of Advent bring to your Christian life?

As you look back over this last year ask yourself how has God used me this year in the lives of others?

What do my resources (time, talent, finances, attitude, thoughts, passions) say about my focus and priorities this past year?

Are you fulfilling the deepest human vocation by learning to serve God by putting other people's needs before your own?

John 13:34-35
"A new command I give you: Love one another. As I have loved you, so you must love one another. By this everyone will know that you are my disciples, if you love one another."

The old is gone and the new is come. You may be more than ready to move into a new year. New opportunities, a fresh start – the new year shines before us like freshly fallen snow with no tracks on it.

Psalm 65:11
"You crown the year with your bounty and your carts overflow with abundance."

Pray

Lord, Whether I leave behind a year of joy or of trials and difficulties, I pause to give thanks.

Thank you for being with me every day of every year.
Thank you for making all things new and for giving me the grace of fresh starts and new beginnings.
Help me to learn from last year and put you at the centre of my life in the year to come.

Looking Back

January

1st January

2 Corinthians 5:17
"Therefore, if anyone is in Christ, he is a new creation. The old has passed away; behold, the new has come".

Jeremiah 29:11
"for I know the plans I have for you," declares the Lord, "plans to prosper you and not to harm you, plans to give you hope and a future."

Spiritual Prompts for the New Year

In which spiritual discipline do I most want to make progress with, this year?

The practice of spiritual disciplines for personal spiritual growth includes Bible study, prayer, meditation, and fasting. These are referred to as inward disciplines. Outward practices are service, solitude, submission, and simplicity, while corporate practices are worship, celebration and guidance.

What's the most important way, by God's grace, I will try to make this year different from last?

What do I want to see God do in my life this coming year?

What areas of my life do I want Him to transform, reshape, or change?

Spending the beginning days and weeks of January mindfully pursuing God's purposes for you in the new year, helps define a clear purpose.

Pray
Loving God, thank You for making all things new.
As another new year begins, help me live each day for You.
May I continually have a new song in my heart to sing to You, no matter what comes my way.
I trust in You because I know that Your mercies are new every morning, and I pray for faith to know that you are always by my side.

Christian Goals for 2025

2nd January

Lamentations 3:22-24

"Because of the Lord's great love we are not consumed, for his compassions never fail. They are new every morning; great is your faithfulness. I say to myself, 'The Lord is my portion; therefore I will wait for him.'"

When a Christian is experiencing a spiritual winter, they can try these practices to nourish their faith:

Engage with God's word: Read the Bible, write songs based on it, or pray while walking.

Remember the blessings God has given you, and embrace the abundance of Christ Jesus.

Making a Difference in 2025

3rd **January**

When a Christian is experiencing a spiritual winter, they can try these practices to nourish their faith:

Spend time alone: Take a walk or sit in silence.

Trust in God: God is at work, even if it doesn't feel like it. He is committed to growing you, and will finish the good work he started in you.

Expect spiritual winters: Prepare for them so they feel less devastating.

4th **January**

Letter 59: Learning to Empty
Castle Weary, Scotland, 4 **January** 2023

I wake up in soft darkness. Today I have the time to do the things I do not usually do. I open the wood-burning stove in the bothy where I am staying. Inside there are still some softly glowing embers from the logs I put in last night. From the porch I take some kindling and push them into the hot ash, lifting them and blowing as I do so. They pop. I blow some more, they pop again and then there is a crackle.

The orange glow intensifies, turns red, and then the first flame licks upwards. I keep blowing and add a log on top. I close the stove door leaving the air vent open as the crackle becomes a soft roar. I remember my father laying a fire meticulously in the front-room grate when I was a child. Balls of newspaper, a scaffolding of kindling and then large lumps of shining coal on top. There is something very satisfying about laying a fire that really burns bright.

Inside the cupboard there is a pack of Italian freshly ground coffee, vacuum packed. I slit it open and watch the ground coffee block crumble. I boil a kettle, listening to the sound of the bubbling water as it comes to the boil. You know the moment the electric kettle will switch off just by the sound.

The morning is very still, just the sound of the bubbling water and the crackle of the firewood, then the gurgle of the water poured over the ground coffee and filling the cafetière. I press down slowly, careful that the scalding coffee does not splash back up in my face. I pour the coffee into a small saucepan and add milk and place it on top of the wood-burning stove. Each of these actions is so pleasing. There is no rush. Outside it is still pitch black. There is no sound apart from the gentle crackle of the fire.

I sit down at the table by the window to write this, and I am so focused on describing the morning that I forget all about the coffee on the stove until I hear the hiss of steam and the sound of the coffee boiling over on to the scorching surface of the stove top, and smell the burnt coffee and milk.

Today I have the time to hear and smell these things, and taste. The coffee tastes delicious. I pull back the curtain that covers the door and open it. The cold winter air rushes in for a moment. I
breathe in – the smell of pine, silver birch, winter and snow. Snow surrounds the bothy. It fell several days ago and in the cold it has frozen over and the edges of the furrows and the footprints are now a latticework of ice. A soft powder of snow is falling now. It is when you have time to notice that the poem begins, liminal and transcendent. The everyday that you never normally notice is astonishing. You become so attentive to the detail that each moment becomes sacramental – filled
with presence and wonder.

Last night, as we drove through the fields of snow, the surface sparkled in the headlights of the car. Five-year old Lyla in the back seat cries out, 'Look, it's glitter dropped by the fairies!' True, it is a glittering field, like crossing a field of diamonds, 'ice crust and snowflake' glistening in the car's lights: 'A polished glancing.

A blue frost-bright dawn.'[1] They drop me off at the bothy, the crunch of the icy snow under my boots. I walk slowly, careful not to slide, breathing in the cold air, sharp as a knife, deep into my London lungs.

I unpack slowly. I am also unpacking the stress and busyness of the last few weeks of Advent and Christmas in London – folding and putting it carefully away.

Ben arrives from across the snow, carefully carrying a hot dish of steak pie with crisp, flaky pastry and small buttery boiled potatoes. I thank him again for picking me up from the station and ask him to pass on my thanks to Amy for the steak pie, and he disappears into the night. After a day on the train without eating, I eat hungrily, the crisp pastry soaking up the thick salty gravy tastes especially delicious.

I shower, a powerful gush of hot Scottish water washing away the city and a day's travel. Then a big white bath towel, stiff and rough from drying in the wind, rubbing my skin like a scouring pad so that it is red and alive. Then I climb into clean white cotton sheets and turn off the light, total blackness enveloping me like a blanket, my buzzing head and body from the city stilling.

It is never dark like this in London, dark as velvet. I remember Amy's words in the car: 'When my dad comes here he says he spends the first seven days just sleeping.' This place has that effect on you. But I can't sleep.

These next hours are like a journey through the night in which I feel my body unknotting, the fibres in my lower back untwisting, the twitches and electricity of the modern city you carry with you without realizing. It's as if you are wired up to the zing of neon. But now I am not just breathing but breathing within. As though right to my marrow I have switched off the human generator of survival and opened myself to the without. I am not anxious about not sleeping. Just growing accustomed to the night.

Meditation now is not something you do but something you are, no longer seeking the stillness but inside the stillness, no longer concentrating on the breath.

You are the breath and the breath is much bigger than you. It is beyond you and filling you with the stillness of the night.

They talk a lot about detox in order to sell manufactured smoothies and health supplements. But perhaps real detoxification needs us to unplug for a while from the consumables that we think power us. Our bodies can become like street bins with rubbish and packaging spilling over and decomposing within.

'Empty', this **January** time says to me. 'Fast. Let your fasting create the space you long for. Clear the clutter. Sweep away the debris. Slow down. Stop. Cough out the virus and breath in the fresh air of winter cleansing.' Like those with consumption who were sent to breathe the mountain air. We talk about the pollution of the planet. Well, pollution begins with our own bodies, which become the dumper trucks. So how about learning to fast again? How about realizing that replenishment does not mean consuming more but less – creating more space to touch, taste, see, smell, recognize, hear.

I am convinced that after Christmas I do not need to be filled any more but emptied. I am convinced we must seek the space between things so that our lives are not just piles of stuff that overwhelm but spaces large enough to see the epiphany, see the stars. We need to create spaces of encounter that belong to no one but make space for all. We can get lost in too much stuff. We do need to bloom where we are planted but we also need to plant where the seed has space and soil to bloom.

I know that in a few days' time the city will draw me back into its frenetic heartbeat. The city is my monastery. And it will not be long before I miss the people and diversity of my home and the community of those who struggle with all the stresses and moans of the modern world and yet can still show such care and grace.

People say there is no community in the city. But I have not found that to be true.

What is in short supply is time – time to see, hear and be generous to those who long for community, and time to process all that takes place.

But when I return to the city, I would like to take back with me this soft blanket of the night, this smell of the winter air, this stillness, even in the midst of the rush, this silent prayer enveloping and quietening the social media of the mind – this time to love and recognize. Make this place, the place you are now, your place of meeting, the place where heaven meets the earth, the place where for a moment all our strivings cease, soft and still and fragrant and tender with the beauty of life. It is only perhaps when we let go of stuff that we find that embrace of the redeemer, but that embrace is worth giving up the whole world for.

When I look at your heavens, the work of your fingers,
the moon and the stars that you have established;
what are human beings that you are mindful of them,
mortals that you care for them?
(Psalm 8.3–4)

Wonderings

I wonder what for you is both ordinary but also astonishing.
I wonder if you can describe any moment in your life that is a sacrament of the present moment.
I wonder what you need to empty.
I wonder, if you create space, what you discover.
I wonder how this year we can make the world a better place.

Note
1 Ted Hughes, 'Icecrust and Snowflake', in Collected Poems of Ted Hughes, ed.
Paul Keegan, London: Faber & Faber, 2012, p. 313.

Richard Carter
Letters from Nazareth: A Contemplative Journey Home

The Nazareth Community, based at London's St Martin in the Fields, is a contemplative community patterned on monastic life for people from all walks of life.

Its rule has seven guiding spiritual principles: Silence, Service, Scripture, Sacrament, Sharing, Sabbath Time and Staying. Founded by Richard Carter in 2018, it now draws members from across the country and from overseas.

Letters are a classic genre of spiritual writing and Richard has written a monthly spiritual letter to the Community since its inception. Collected here, his letters aim to encourage readers to live out a simple rule of life, to reflect, pray and live with compassion despite the challenges of modern life.

Rich in biblical reflection, poetic meditation and practical guidance for living in demanding times, Letters from Nazareth abounds in simple yet profound wisdom for our world today.

Thoughts and Prayers

Winter reflections

Bible Verses

Hopes and Fears

How can I be a good and faithful servant?

5th **January**

When a Christian is experiencing a spiritual winter, they can try these practices to nourish their faith:

Be confident: God is not in a hurry, and you can trust that he is working even if it's not on your preferred timeline.

Winter can be a time when God's work is happening, even if it doesn't feel like it. It can also be a time to build trust in God and develop into a better person.

6th January
Epiphany

What does the word "Epiphany" mean?
'Epiphany' comes from Greek and means 'to show', referring to Jesus being revealed or shown to the world as God's beloved Son. The six Sundays which follow Epiphany are called the 'time of manifestation'.

What is the Feast of the Epiphany about?
Epiphany is the feast that celebrates the beginning of the revelation of the significance and importance of Jesus Christ while still a baby to the Three Wise Men (the Magi) who had travelled from the East to Bethlehem.

When do we celebrate the Feast of the Epiphany?
Epiphany, or the 12th day of Christmas, falls on the 6th of **January** in the West and marks the official end of Christmas.

Matthew 2: 1-23

The Visit of the Wise Men
2 Now after Jesus was born in Bethlehem of Judea in the days of Herod the king, behold, wise men from the east came to Jerusalem, 2 saying, "Where is he who has been born king of the Jews? For we saw his star when it rose and have come to worship him." 3 When Herod the king heard this, he was troubled, and all Jerusalem with him; 4 and assembling all the chief priests and scribes of the people, he inquired of them where the Christ was to be born. 5 They told him, "In Bethlehem of Judea, for so it is written by the prophet:6
"'And you, O Bethlehem, in the land of Judah,
are by no means least among the rulers of Judah; for from you shall come a ruler who will shepherd my people Israel.'"

7 Then Herod summoned the wise men secretly and ascertained from them what time the star had appeared. 8 And he sent them to Bethlehem, saying, "Go and search diligently for the child, and when you have found him, bring me word, that I too may come and worship him." 9 After listening to the king, they went on their way. And behold, the star that they had seen when it rose went before

them until it came to rest over the place where the child was. 10 When they saw the star, they rejoiced exceedingly with great joy. 11 And going into the house, they saw the child with Mary his mother, and they fell down and worshiped him. Then, opening their treasures, they offered him gifts, gold and frankincense and myrrh.

12 And being warned in a dream not to return to Herod, they departed to their own country by another way.

The Flight to Egypt
13 Now when they had departed, behold, an angel of the Lord appeared to Joseph in a dream and said, "Rise, take the child and his mother, and flee to Egypt, and remain there until I tell you, for Herod is about to search for the child, to destroy him." 14 And he rose and took the child and his mother by night and departed to Egypt 15 and remained there until the death of Herod. This was to fulfil what the Lord had spoken by the prophet, "Out of Egypt I called my son."

Herod Kills the Children
16 Then Herod, when he saw that he had been tricked by the wise men, became furious, and he sent and killed all the male children in Bethlehem and in all that region who were two years old or under, according to the time that he had ascertained from the wise men. 17 Then was fulfilled what was spoken by the prophet Jeremiah:18 "A voice was heard in Ramah, weeping and loud lamentation, Rachel weeping for her children; she refused to be comforted, because they are no more."

The Return to Nazareth
19 But when Herod died, behold, an angel of the Lord appeared in a dream to Joseph in Egypt, 20 saying, "Rise, take the child and his mother and go to the land of Israel, for those who sought the child's life are dead." 21 And he rose and took the child and his mother and went to the land of Israel. 22 But when he heard that Archelaus was reigning over Judea in place of his father Herod, he was afraid to go there, and being warned in a dream he withdrew to the district of Galilee. 23 And he went and lived in a city called Nazareth, so that what was spoken by the prophets might be fulfilled, that he would be called a Nazarene.

Pray

God of Advent, Christmas and Epiphany, you have given me many signs and prophecies
about your Son Jesus Christ's birth, and they have been fulfilled.
May I see from the past to the present, the present into the future, that your loving hand guides all things.

Loving God, you know my situation. You know me so well. Even the number of hairs on my head.

As the Good Shepherd, lead me to green pastures and still waters, restoring my soul and nurturing my spirit. Let me find solace and strength.

May the light of Your love shine upon me, illuminating my path and lifting me from the darkness of despair. Grant me hope and resilience as I journey through life's challenges.

Please God, show me how to be a good and faithful servant this year.

7th January

Isaiah 1:18
"Come now, let us reason together, says the Lord: though your sins are like scarlet, they shall be as white as snow; though they are red like crimson, they shall become like wool.

When a Christian is experiencing a spiritual winter, they can try these spiritual practices to nourish their faith:

Prayer: Prayer can help you feel peace and clarity. You can pray for God's will, guidance, or your future goals.

Journaling: Writing in a journal can help you reflect on your thoughts, check in with yourself, and identify patterns of behaviour.

Read scripture: You can pray for God to speak to you through scripture and give you the knowledge to understand what he is laying on your heart.

Attend spiritual retreats: Retreats can help us deepen our faith and build connections.

Worship: Worship is a way to nurture our relationship with faith.

Social action: Social action is a way to nurture our relationship with faith.

8th **January**

Winter Prayer Walking

Destination Praying

Releasing. On the way to your destination or in the early part of your walk, let go of what's on your mind. Shed your thoughts and distractions. Open your heart to God and quiet your mind.

Receiving. When you reach your destination, stay as long as you like. Continue to open your heart and quiet your mind. Receive what is there for you to receive.

Returning. As you follow the same path back to your beginning point, offer yourself to God, resting in God's presence with you.

9th January

Isaiah 55:10

"For as the rain and the snow come down from heaven and do not return there but water the earth, making it bring forth and sprout, giving seed to the sower and bread to the eater,

10th **January**

God Provides For Our Needs in Winter

Proverbs 31:21
When it snows, she has no fear for her household; for all of them are clothed in scarlet [wool].

Sometimes thoughts of winter bring forth fears of being caught in a blinding snowstorm or of freezing to death outside in the cold conditions.

God always provides everything we need as we experience the harsh cold of winter.

Winter is a wonderful time to be especially grateful that we have a home to shelter us from storms and for the warm clothes we have to wear and good hot food to eat.

Let us thank God for all the blessings He has poured into our lives to prepare us and strengthen us for the difficult conditions we face.

Let us thank God for being our refuge and strength in winter so that we have nothing to fear as we face each day.

11th January

Psalm 130:5
" I wait for the Lord, my whole being waits, and in his word I put my hope."

This is what winter offers: roots strong and deep and secure in the hope of waiting on our God to come through.

12th **January**

Winter Prayer Walk

Praying while walking

Isaiah 40:31

"But those who hope in the Lord will renew their strength. They will soar on wings like eagles; they will run and not grow weary, they will walk and not be faint."

Begin by inviting God into your walk.

"Lord, walk with me and guide my thoughts and prayers."

Once we have begun to let prayer enter into us and filter into our very flesh and blood, then we begin to pray wherever we are. Our prayer becomes our response and compassion for the world.

Many of us experience the need for space and yet we don't know how to find it. Too often our space is crowded out by the fillers that leave us depleted and empty.

Take your prayers outside as we learn to walk and talk with Jesus on the road and in nature.

Life is dominated with so many distractions, the news on repeat, checking emails, the ping of another message, the scrolling that can occupy our soul and take us hostage, the anxieties, the worries - 'For most of my life I have been worrying about things that never happen'.

Proverbs 3:5-6

"Trust in the Lord with all your heart and lean not on your own understanding; in all your ways submit to him, and he will make your paths straight."

Then there are ;

The addictions which imprison us

The unforgiven resentment that festers

The relationship or disagreement that hurts like an unhealed wound

The sin that still haunts

The crowded mind

The occupied heart

The trapped life.

Each day we need to find space to walk with God

'Follow me,' he says

To look

To hear

To touch

To breathe in

To catch the scent of God's season.

So open your door and go in search of space

Let your walking become your prayer

Let your breathing in and out become your gift and your offering

Look up and out

Feel the earth

Smell the rain

The shiver of the cold

The warmth of the sun

The gust of wind unbalancing you

See the sky

The shape and movement of the clouds

The position of the sun

The movement of the trees

The colour, the shape, the light, the shadow of the leaves and branches

Watch for the messengers of grace, they will come when you are least expecting.

13th January

Philippians 4:6–7

Do not be anxious about anything, but in every situation, by prayer and petition, with thanksgiving, present your requests to God. And the peace of God, which transcends all understanding, will guard your hearts and your minds in Christ Jesus.

Psalm 34:4–5, 8

I sought the LORD, and He answered me and delivered me from all my fears. Those who look to Him are radiant, and their faces shall never be ashamed. Oh, taste and see that the LORD is good! Blessed is the man who takes refuge in Him!

14th **January**

The winter of the soul

Psalm 130:5 – 6
In the winter of his soul the psalmist wrote, "I wait for the Lord, my soul waits, and in His word I put my hope.
My soul waits for the Lord more than watchmen wait for the morning"

The most difficult season of the soul for most is winter.

The winter of the soul is bleak, cold, dark, and fruitless. We lack the energy to engage in activities that just recently filled us with joy.

Winter is a season of unwelcome brooding, often late at night, robbing us of sleep. Most things feel dead, or appear to be so.

The days are short, the nights stretch on and on.

Winter never seems to end.

15th January

Psalm 147:16-18 – God Sends His Word and Melts Ice
"He gives snow like wool; he scatters frost like ashes. He hurls down his crystals of ice like crumbs; who can stand before his cold? He sends out his word, and melts them; he makes his wind blow and the waters flow."

This Psalm vividly describes God's power over the winter elements. It serves as a reminder that God is in control of all circumstances in our lives, including the most challenging and seemingly insurmountable 'winters'.

16th January

Thriving in the Winter Season of the Soul
Does God seem silent?
Are your dreams and visions for the future lifeless and not coming to fruition?
Have your plans been disrupted and now you are on a different path than you wanted to be?
Has your health caused you to slow down and not be as active?

17th January

Matthew 6:31–34

"So do not worry, saying, 'What shall we eat?' or 'What shall we drink?' or "What shall we wear?' For the pagans run after all these things, and your heavenly Father knows that you need them. But seek first His kingdom and His righteousness, and all these things will be given to you as well. Therefore do not worry about tomorrow, for tomorrow will worry about itself. Each day has enough trouble of its own."

Proverbs 3:5–6

Trust in the LORD with all your heart, and do not lean on your own understanding. In all your ways acknowledge Him, and He will make straight your paths.

18th January

Isaiah 28:2 – The Lord is a Crown of Glory
"Behold, the Lord has one who is mighty and strong; like a storm of hail, a destroying tempest, like a storm of mighty, overflowing waters, he casts down to the earth with his hand."

Romans 15:13
May the God of hope fill you with all joy and peace as you trust in Him, so that you may overflow with hope by the power of the Holy Spirit.

19th **January**

Isaiah 41:10

"Don't be afraid, for I am with you.

Don't be discouraged, for I am your God.

I will strengthen you and help you.

I will hold you up with my victorious right hand."

20th **January**

2 Timothy 4:21 – Paul's Request to Timothy
"Do your best to get here before winter…"

Paul's request to Timothy to visit him before winter reflects the urgency and the challenges that winter could pose for travel and communication. This can be seen as a metaphor for making the most of the opportunities we have before facing harder times, much like winter.

21st January

Snow Points to the Glory of God

Daniel 7:9
"As I looked, thrones were set in place, and the Ancient of Days took his seat. His clothing was as white as snow; the hair of his head was white like wool. His throne was flaming with fire, and its wheels were all ablaze.

The dazzling white nature of snow is a shadow of the glorious nature of God that will be revealed to us in heaven. The full glory of Christ our Lord is truly brighter and more magnificent than our eyes can see or our minds can imagine, but the clothing of Jesus Christ and even His hair is often likened to the white of snow.

The pure, white appearance of snow can remind us of the purity and holiness of God, whom one day we will see face to face.

22nd January

Silent Retreat
We came inside and it was spring
Leaving the fresh snow outside
Its soft white blanket marking our footsteps to the door
And silencing the din of our lives
As we discovered Focolare
The hearth and place of warmth
A generosity of welcome that received us
And gave us their place as though it were our own
I pulled up the blinds to let the light in
An open and spacious place
With clean soft colours
Yellows, whites and olives
A simple circle of chairs
Daffodils in three pottery jugs
Opening signs of spring
And spring in our hearts too
As we let go of our defences and controls
And let God expand in us
At times as thrilling, chilling and as life-giving
As a gulp of winter air
As dazzling as snow covering the earth
Yet as warm as a fireside with windows and doors that open out and welcome in.
How can we learn from you and be this hearth too
This fire of God's Spirit that radiates warmth
How can we create a space to live with generous hospitality and attentiveness?
A pattern and way of life that creates both space and acceptance
Belonging and yet freedom
Expectation and yet mercy
Warmth without shutting out the mystery of this fall of snow
We found true hospitality here
That got out of the way but was still present with us
And allowed buds to open
While still rejoicing in the wonder of winter outside.

Richard Carter

The City is my Monastery – A contemporary rule of life.
'Our place of retreat, our monastery, is here and now, where we are today'

23rd January

Jeremiah 36:22 – The King in Winter
"It was the ninth month and the king was sitting in the winter apartment, with a fire burning in the firepot in front of him."

This verse describes a scene of comfort and warmth during winter in the king's house. It can be seen as a metaphor for God's provision and warmth during our own 'winter seasons' – times when we may feel cold and distant, God provides a haven of warmth and comfort.

24th January
God Established Seasons as Boundaries
Psalm 74:17
It was You who set all the boundaries of the earth; You made both summer and winter.

It is clear that God very purposefully made both summer and winter (and springtime and autumn). The seasons are part of His divine established order in the universe, creating rules and boundaries under which the natural world must operate.

There is a purpose and time for rest and hibernation of winter, just as the growth and refreshment of summer.

Although He permits for temperatures, plant life, and sunlight patterns to change throughout the year, there is a cyclical pattern of life in which the snow will not forever cover the ground or the blazing sun will not always burn.

There are boundaries to each season of life.

Enjoy the blessings of winter while it lasts.

25th **January**
In Philippians 4:11-13, the apostle Paul says: …I have learned to be content whatever the circumstances. I know what it is to be in need, and I know what it is to have plenty. I have learned the secret of being content in any and every situation, whether well fed or hungry, whether living in plenty or in want. I can do all this through him who gives me strength.

26th **January**

Romans 8:28
And we know that for those who love God all things work together for good, for those who are called according to His purpose.

Joshua 1:9
"Have I not commanded you? Be strong and courageous. Do not be frightened, and do not be dismayed, for the LORD your God is with you wherever you go."

27th **January**

2 Corinthians 5:7
 "For we live by faith, not by sight."

Psalm 23: 5-6
 "You prepare a table before me in the presence of my enemies. You anoint my head with oil; my cup overflows. Surely your goodness and love will follow me all the days of my life, and I will dwell in the house of the LORD for ever."

1 John 4:4
"You, dear children, are from God and have overcome them, because the one who is in you is greater than the one who is in the world."

28th January

Winter Prayer Walking
Let's go for a walk

Psalm 37 -23

The LORD makes firm the steps of the one who delights in him;

Prayer walking can take many forms.

It can be a time to be outside and experience the wonder of God in nature.

It can be a time to walk around a neighbourhood and pray people and the community through intercessional prayer.

It can be a time of personal reflection where you review your day or the last time you went for a prayer walk.

It can be a time of creative prayer where you walk and pray the psalms or bible verses that you have committed to memory.

Jeremiah 29:11

God has a path for your feet to follow, a plan for your heart to discover, and a purpose for your life to fulfil

29th **January**

Psalm 147:16-18 – God Sends His Word and Melts Ice
"He gives snow like wool; he scatters frost like ashes. He hurls down his crystals of ice like crumbs; who can stand before his cold? He sends out his word, and melts them; he makes his wind blow and the waters flow."

30th January

Ephesians 6:10
"Finally, be strengthened by the Lord and his powerful strength."

John 15:4
"Remain in me, as I also remain in you. No branch can bear fruit by itself; it must remain in the vine. Neither can you bear fruit unless you remain in me."

31st January

Christ be my Light

Longing for light, I wait in darkness.

Longing for truth, I turn to you.

Make me your own light for the world to see.

Christ, be my light!

Shine in my heart.

Shine through the darkness.

Christ, be my light!

Looking Back

February

1st February

The winter of the soul

Psalm 130:5 – 6
In the winter of his soul the psalmist wrote, "I wait for the Lord, my soul waits, and in His word I put my hope.
My soul waits for the Lord more than watchmen wait for the morning"

In winter we are tempted to question our faith, to doubt our value.

With nothing to show, no "fruit," no productivity, no outward activity to speak of, we feel as though our worth has shrivelled to nothing.

God is silent.

Friends drift away.

The ground goes fallow.

All we can do is wait and pray.

2nd February

There are several Bible verses about peace that can provide comfort during difficult times.

Psalm 31:1-2

"In you, Lord, I have taken refuge; let me never be put to shame; deliver me in your righteousness. Turn your ear to me, come quickly to my rescue; be my rock of refuge, a strong fortress to save me."

Psalm 46:1-3
"God is our refuge and strength, an ever-present help in trouble. Therefore we will not fear, though the earth give way and the mountains fall into the heart of the sea, though its waters roar and foam and the mountains quake with their surging."

3rd February

Winter Prayer Walking

Prayer Walking Guide

Here is a step by step guide to prayer walking:

Find a location:

Set an intention: Before you begin walking, take a moment to set an intention for your prayer walk. This could be a specific issue or concern you want to pray for, or a general desire to connect more deeply with God and the world around you.

Start walking: Begin walking at a slow, comfortable pace. Take deep breaths and try to relax any tension in your body.

Observe your surroundings: As you walk, take notice of your surroundings. Look for areas that seem in need of prayer, or that inspire feelings of gratitude and joy.

Pray as you walk: As you continue walking, begin to pray out loud or silently. You can pray for the needs of yourself, your loved ones, your community, or the world at large. You can also simply offer prayers of gratitude or praise.

Listen for guidance: As you pray, try to be open and receptive to any insights or guidance that come to you. Listen for God's voice and trust that He will lead you in the right direction.

Be present: As you walk, try to stay present in the moment. Don't worry about the future or dwell on the past. Instead, focus on the beauty and wonder of the present moment.

Close with gratitude: When you are finished with your walk, take a few moments to express gratitude for the experience. Thank God for His presence, His guidance, and His blessings.

Remember, a prayer walk is not about distance or number of prayers. It is about connecting with God and seeking His guidance and blessings.

Always walk with an open heart, ready to connect with God's love and grace.

After a prayer walk, you can reflect on what you noticed, how you felt, and when you felt God's presence.

4th February
Job 37:9-10
From its chamber comes the whirlwind, and cold from the scattering winds. By the breath of God ice is given, and the broad waters are frozen fast.

Psalm 74:17
You have fixed all the boundaries of the earth; you have made summer and winter.

5th February
Decision-Making in Winter
Acts 27:12
"Since the harbour was unsuitable to winter in, the majority decided that we should sail on, hoping to reach Phoenix and winter there..."

This verse from Acts describes a practical decision made to face winter in a more suitable place. It can be seen as a metaphor for the decisions we make in life, seeking God's guidance to find the right 'harbour' during our difficult seasons.

6th February

The winter of the soul can be a time of spiritual dormancy, introspection, and waiting.

It can be a time of feeling cold, dark, and fruitless, and lacking the energy to do things that were once enjoyable. However, the winter of the soul can also be a time of learning, healing, and preparation for a spiritual spring.

The winter of the soul can be a time to:
Deepen roots
Nurture seeds
Anticipate a future harvest
Prepare for the soft ground of spring
Cultivate and grow new things
Find God
Pray your broken pieces back into wholeness

Think about

Solitude.
Learn to be alone.
Take long walks.
Sit in silence.
Schedule time with Jesus and leave your phone at home.
Get away by yourself for a day.
Be present to God in the silence so that you can be present to people in the noise.

7th February

Looking ahead to Lent

Lent is the time before Easter which calls us into self-examination as well as self-denial. We look inward to appraise our inner spiritual life. We make an evaluation of where we are in our relationship with God.

Lent can take various forms, but commonly they involve prayer, repentance, and service. We spend more time in prayer, try to become less self-absorbed through self-denial and seek deliberately to be of greater help to others.

8th February

Romans 15:13
May the God of hope fill you with all joy and peace in believing, so that you will abound in hope by the power of the Holy Spirit.

Psalm 118:14
"The LORD is my strength and my defence; he has become my salvation."

9th February

Isaiah 40:31
"…but those who hope in the LORD will renew their strength. They will soar on wings like eagles; they will run and not grow weary, they will walk and not be faint."

Philippians 4:13
"I can do all this through him who gives me strength."

10th February

The Winter of the Soul

Psalm 130:5 – 6
In the winter of his soul the psalmist wrote, "I wait for the Lord, my soul waits, and in His word I put my hope.
My soul waits for the Lord more than watchmen wait for the morning"

God is not in a hurry.

This is about God's time not our time.

When we feel that it is God's job to respond quickly to our every request, we are on a fast track to disillusionment.

Unless our waiting is shaped by the confidence that God is at work, the perceived delay will debilitate us.

The season of winter encourages the development of patience and of a confident trust that God is at work even if he is not operating within our preferred time frame.

11th February

Psalm 42:11

"Why am I discouraged? Why is my heart so sad? I will put my hope in God! I will praise him again—my Savior and my God!"

What keeps you up at night or what consumes your thoughts?

God knows your struggles and He cares very deeply.

Put your hope in God no matter how helpless the situation feels.

He is trustworthy and will sustain you.

2 Corinthians 1:3-5
"Praise be to the God and Father of our Lord Jesus Christ, the Father of compassion and the God of all comfort, who comforts us in all our troubles, so that we can comfort those in any trouble with the comfort we ourselves have received from God"

12th February

Joshua 1:9
"Have I not commanded you? Be strong and courageous. Do not be afraid; do not be discouraged, for the Lord your God will be with you wherever you go.

Isaiah 41:10
"So do not fear, for I am with you; do not be dismayed, for I am your God. I will strengthen you and help you; I will uphold you with my righteous right hand."

13th February

Letter 8: A Letter Home from Ugo

February 2020

Dear Mum,

I have been in the UK for 11 years now. It's not easy since I came here because of my health. I have been in and out of hospital a lot. My sickle-cell anaemia causes a lot of pain, especially when it's cold like now. I am in hospital at the moment.

I didn't want to tell you, Mum, as I know you will get worried, but I am still homeless. It's hard and lonely and makes me depressed – the cold, the wet, no place to call my own. It's worse at the moment because it's winter.

There are also a lot of things I fear on the streets, like drugs and alcohol and fighting and many hardships.

But, Mum, you will be pleased – since I started coming to St Martin's I have found God. This church is so welcoming. I get support from everyone in the International Group. The Nazareth Community has become my family. I love them very much. I help steward in the church, and read the Bible lessons in public. I also act in the Christmas drama – it makes me happy because I belong.
I always think of Nigeria. I miss you, Mum, and my brothers and sisters. It is because of you that I am a Christian. I cannot forget that when I was young you taught me to pray, waking me every day at 5.30 a.m. for morning devotion. Those prayers really help me now. I miss your cooking too! I want you to keep praying for me so everything will go well. Do not forget that I am still your son.

My love and prayers
Your son
Ugo

Richard Carter
Letters from Nazareth: A Contemplative Journey Home

14th February

Thriving in the Winter Season of the Soul

Isaiah 40:31
"But those who trust in the Lord will find new strength.

They will soar high on wings like eagles.

They will run and not grow weary.

They will walk and not faint."

15th February

Thriving in the Winter Season of the Soul

Proverbs 3:5-6
Trust in the Lord with all your heart; do not depend on your own understanding.
Seek His will in all you do, and He will show you which path to take.

Observation
Winter prayer walking involves observing the world around you with an open mind, and asking the Holy Spirit to speak to you through what you see.

16th February

Hebrews 11:1
"Now faith is confidence in what we hope for and assurance about what we do not see."

Romans 15:13
"May the God of hope fill you with all joy and peace as you trust in him, so that you may overflow with hope by the power of the Holy Spirit."

Hebrews 6:19
"We have this hope as an anchor for the soul, firm and secure."

17th February

Psalm 28:7

"The Lord is my strength and shield.

I trust him with all my heart.

He helps me, and my heart is filled with joy.

I burst out in songs of thanksgiving."

18th February

Philippians 2:3–4
Do nothing from selfish ambition or conceit, but in humility count others more significant than yourselves. Let each of you look not only to his own interests, but also to the interests of others.

Psalm 94:18–19
When I thought, "My foot slips," Your steadfast love, O LORD, helped me up. When the cares of my heart are many, Your consolations cheer my soul.

19th February

Even now, declares the Lord, 'return to me with all your heart'. Joel 2:12

At times Lent can be hard going. Its self-appraisal does not come easily. We may pay lip service to Lent on a superficial level, but if we go deeper it will hurt however we will be rewarded with the prize of having God come and dwell in our midst.

If we want to dig deeper into Lent then we should use prayer, penance, and service, not as burdens to be borne, but as keys to joy, ways of unlocking doors to happiness, for each one can lead us to a deeper awareness of the divine presence.

20th February

Lent is a time when Christians journey towards Easter. We try to turn away from doing wrong, we try to turn back and ask God to help us become more like Jesus in how we treat other people and our world. The word Lent in English comes from the "lengthening" of the hours of daylight and the theme is of penitence.

What do you need to repent of?
God's grace is abundant and there is nothing that He cannot forgive. Take time reflecting on where you have turned away from God, tell God about it.

Pray that God would help you see his image in every person you meet.

In the evening, spend a few minutes reviewing the day.
Who did you meet God in?
Who did you struggle with?

Lent Prompts

What does the Lord require of me during Lent?

How can I to use these days of Lent to strengthen my faith?

What are my Lenten goals?

What do I need to turn away from?

What blocks me from turning back to God?

What do I need to do to turn back to God?

Revelation 21:4

"He will wipe away every tear from their eyes, and death shall be no more, neither shall there be mourning, nor crying, nor pain anymore, for the former things have passed away." And He who was seated on the throne said, "Behold, I am making all things new."

21st February

Winter Prayer Walking

You can use your prayer walk as a time of reflection

REPLAY

Think through the events of your day, or the time since your previous moment of reflection. What took place as you replay events in your mind? How did you feel? What emotions do you notice? In which moments did you recognise God's presence?

REJOICE

Take time to worship Jesus, thanking Him for how He revealed His goodness in both obvious and the unseen. What are you grateful for?

REPENT

Bring to mind how you may have wronged God in thought, word and deed, by what you have done and left undone. Consider the moments where you have not loved God with your whole heart and settled for lesser loves; or the moments when you have neglected others. Say sorry to your loving Father as you confess and move towards repentance as you receive His boundless forgiveness and choose to live in the direction of His Kingdom.

RESOLVE

Close your time of reflection by prayerfully committing to live the Christ life, in the Christ way as you look to the future. Ask that you may become more aware of God's presence in every moment of your day.

22nd February

Lent is six weeks that are set apart for the purpose of drawing closer to God and seeking him with greater intensity.

Unfortunately, the Lenten season often gets reduced to the question,

"What are you giving up for Lent?"

This is a fine question, but it can only take us so far. The real question of the Lenten season is, "How will I repent and return to God with all my heart?"

This leads on to an even deeper question: "Where in my life have I gotten away from God, and what are the disciplines that will enable me to find my way back?"

Hope

Each day is an opportunity for hope

And hope will often arise from those deemed hopeless

Learn to hope in God even when hope seems impossible and beyond

Learn to hope in God's grace even when the rules of the world cry out that your values have no currency

Learn to hope in God's love

Hope as tender and ephemeral as a new shoot

But which can make the desert bloom and song birds return

Richard Carter
Letters from Nazareth: A Contemplative Journey Home

23rd February

With prayer and fasting, self-examination and repentance, forgiving others as we have been forgiven, and storing up treasure in heaven by giving generously to others, we can develop spiritual practices of Lent that will help to open our hearts to God.

Philippians 4:8

"And now, dear brothers and sisters, one final thing. Fix your thoughts on what is true, and honourable, and right, and pure, and lovely, and admirable. Think about things that are excellent and worthy of praise."

Doubt. Fear. Worry. Judgment. These are all things we can fix our minds on. But, it is not life giving in any way. It pulls us down further into the winter blues.

Instead, let's fix our minds on what is true, and honourable, and right, and pure, and lovely, and admirable. How do we do that?

Name the other thought out loud and ask Jesus to fill your mind with His truth.

Read God's word and find comfort.

We will see and feel a difference in our attitude and mindsets.

24th February

John 16:33
"In the world you will have tribulation. But take heart; I have overcome the world."

Isaiah 41:10
"So do not fear, for I am with you; do not be dismayed, for I am your God. I will strengthen you and help you; I will uphold you with my righteous right hand."

During a spiritual winter, it can feel like God has abandoned us and like the dryness of our spirit will never come to an end.

The persistent darkness and feelings of loneliness can leave us feeling confused and discouraged.

Periods of cold, silence, and waiting are never easy to go through but they are a necessary part of our journey with God.

So how do we survive the spiritual winters of our lives? We must hold onto the hope of Christ, walking by faith when we cannot see. It is important to remember that God has not changed even when you experience a time of barrenness.

25th February

Lent

Take some time to reflect on the place in your life where you feel distant from God. What has distracted you from cultivating your relationship with God more intentionally?

Begin your Lenten journey by saying something honest to God and reflecting on what you might "give up" or rearrange in order to create more space and passion for this most important relationship.

Decide to spend five minutes every day in silence as your Lenten prayer practice. Wrestle with quieting your mind. Learn that communicating with God can be as simple as resting in His presence.

Pray
Loving God, let something essential happen to me this Lent.
Let me understand what I need to do to turn back to you.
Gracious God speak to my condition this Lent and change me in ways that matter.
Be by my side through Lent and let me see you more clearly.
Show me what is blocking my relationship with you.
Open my eyes and heart to the impediments that exist between us.
Please grant me a willing spirit to return to you with all my heart.

Psalm 147:16
He gives snow like wool; he scatters frost like ashes.

Psalm 51:7
Purge me with hyssop, and I shall be clean; wash me, and I shall be whiter than snow.

Christ is our hope to weather this season, but it is important to firmly cling to the fact that the winter of the soul will not last forever. God alone appoints the time we need to remain in a spiritual winter, but there is no doubt that the cold, isolation, and silence of winter will come to an end.

26th February

Psalm 148:7-8
Praise the Lord from the earth, you great sea creatures and all deeps, fire and hail, snow and mist, stormy wind fulfilling his word!

God is the good, loving, compassionate, and faithful God He has always been. During the winter of the soul He is calling you to deeper intimacy with Him, trusting Him to provide and sustain you through difficult days, rewarding you with a hope that endures.

The night of winter is an open door inviting you to experience God's love in a much deeper and more profound way as you come face to face with your desperation for His Presence.

27th February

Deuteronomy 31:8
"Do not be afraid or discouraged, for the Lord will personally go ahead of you. He will be with you; he will neither fail you nor abandon you."

Whatever you are facing right now, be encouraged to take hold of this promise in a fresh way.
God is here, He is ahead of you and God is holding you close.
He will never leave you.
You can walk in boldness and confidence today.

Embrace the season of winter for the profound lessons God is teaching you and the ways in which you feel His intimate embrace that sustains you in the darkness. And then cling to the hope of knowing that spring is just around the corner, and it will be a glorious time of rejoicing in the new things that are springing forth from your life. Glory to God!

28th February

Spring and Singing Are Coming

Song of Songs 2:11-12

See! The winter is past; the rains are over and gone. Flowers appear on the earth; the season of singing has come
Spring will burst forth; new growth will arise in glorious rejoicing. Beautiful, colourful flowers will display the splendour of God's glory, and singing will fill your soul and spirit. The treasures of embracing the joys of life once more become so much more precious after overcoming the adversities of a difficult winter. May you be filled with overflowing praises to God for the goodness and faithfulness of God.

Looking Back

What have you learnt about your relationship with God?

What will you take forward with you in your relationship with God?

Preparing for Lent

If daily readings aid your Christian journey then the next event in the Christian calendar is Lent.

Lent is a time of 40 days when we open ourselves up to God for his examination.

Lent is a season that prepares our hearts for the celebration of Easter, much like Advent prepares us for Christmas.

In 2025, Lent is from Ash Wednesday on 5th March 2025 to Easter Sunday 20th April 2025

Feedback

There are free eBooks to download for 5 days from Sunday 2nd March 2025 at Lent Publications on Amazon.

There are free prayer eBooks to download from Lent Publications on Amazon on 1st **December**, 1st June and 1st September.

Please follow Lent Publications on Amazon.

Type into your search engine browser

Amazon author page lent publications

Please leave a positive review.

Printed in Dunstable, United Kingdom